Marshall Cavendish

P9-DCU-773

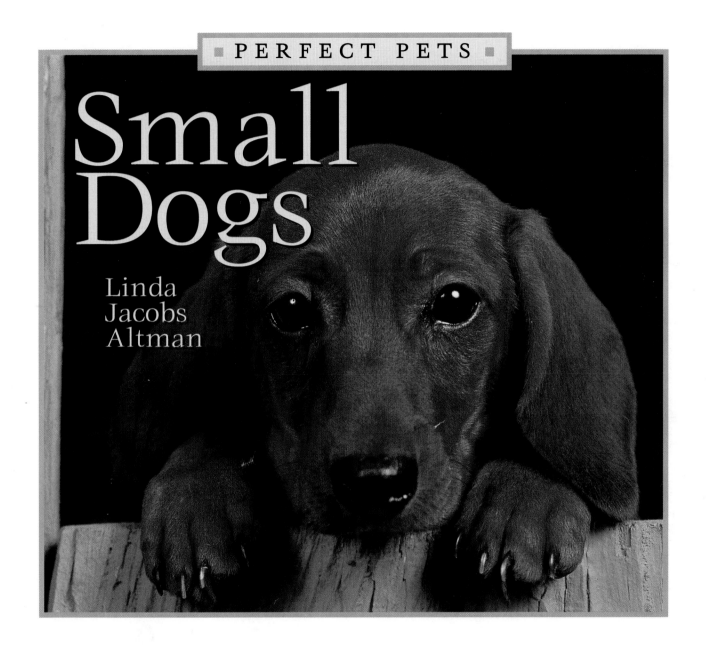

PERFECT PETS

Small Dogs

Linda
Jacobs
Altman

BENCHMARK BOOKS

MARSHALL CAVENDISH

NEW YORK

Benchmark Books
Marshall Cavendish Corporation
99 White Plains Road
Tarrytown, New York 10591

© 1999 by Marshall Cavendish Corporation

Library of Congress Cataloging-in-Publication Data
Altman, Linda Jacobs, date
Small dogs / by Linda Jacobs Altman.
p.   cm. — (Perfect pets)
Includes bibliographical references (p.   ).
Summary: Describes the characteristics and behavior of small dogs in general, also discussing the physical appearance and place in history of some specific breeds.
ISBN 0-7614-0795-2
1. Dogs—Juvenile literature. [1. Dogs.] I. Title. II. Series.
SF426.5.A5   1999   636.7—DC21   97-40463   CIP   AC

Photo research by Matthew and Ellen Dudley

Cover photo: *Photo Researchers, Inc.:* Frederic/Jacana
Back cover photo: *Norvia Behling*

The photographs in this book are used by permission and through the courtesy of: # 1457 Department of Library Services, American Museum of Natural History, 4; *Animals Animals:* Gérard Lacz, 3; Robert & Eunice Pearcy, 6; Robert Pearcy, 16; *Norvia Behling:* 7, 14, 15, 17 (top), 20, 22, 24, 25; *Earth Scenes:* Robert & Eunice Pearcy, 8; *Photo Researchers, Inc.:* Jose Dupont/ Jacana, 1; Renee Lynn, 9; Jeanne White, 10, 13 (top); R. Van Nostrand, 12; Herbert Kehrer/OKAPIA, 13 (bottom); Mary Eleanor Browning, 17 (bottom); Catherine Ursillo, 18; Mero/ Jacana, 21; Susan Leavikes, 23; Bildarchiv/OKAPIA, 26 (top); Susan Kuklin, 26 (bottom); Margaret Miller, 28; Tim Davis, 29; Fredrick Ayer, 30; *Photofest:* 27.

Printed in Hong Kong
6   5   4   3   2   1

In memory of Ezekiel,
who always tried to be
the biggest, baddest Westie
on the block

The Chihuahua's long history goes back to ancient Mexico. Its ancestors were called Techichi by the Toltec people. This statue of a Techichi is in the American Museum of Natural History.

Small dogs

make great pets. They also make good friends. Like their larger cousins, they are loyal, loving, and smart. Though most of them could fit into a tote bag or a bicycle basket, they pack a lot of energy into those little bodies.

Many small **breeds** have found a place in history and legend. More than a thousand years ago, the Toltec people of Mexico honored the graceful Chihuahua (Chee-WAH-wah). Stone carvings of these tiny dogs have been found in ancient temples. Their skeletons also have been found buried with honor in human graves.

In Tibet, little dogs with long, golden hair guarded the great temple at Lhasa (LAH-sah). If a stranger came near, they set up a terrific barking. If a friend came, they welcomed him with wagging tails. They always seemed to know the difference.

The coat of this Lhasa apso is the original color for the breed. It is called "golden." Goldens can be many different shades, from palest cream to the color of thick, clover honey.

The monks called them Lhasa apsos, the "lions" of Lhasa. They proved that size isn't everything, even for a watchdog.

Dogs sense danger in ways we do not understand. A tiny papillon (pap-ee-YON) once tried to save the life of King Henri III of France. In French, the word papillon means "butterfly." The name fits the breed. Papillons have beautiful ears, which look like butterfly wings.

King Henri had several papillons. He liked to put them in open baskets and take them along wherever he went. They were quiet and well behaved. Then one day the king's favorite papillon started barking at a royal advisor. Nothing anybody did could stop her. She barked and barked until the king had her taken out of the room.

The dainty appearance of this papillon is part of its charm. The face mask and the fringed ears make the "butterfly" effect.

A short time later, the advisor stabbed the king. Nobody knew how that little dog had sensed the danger.

Besides sensing things that humans miss, dogs are known for their loyalty. In Scotland, people still tell the story of a little terrier named Bobby. His master died and was buried in Greyfriars Cemetery. Bobby kept watch over the grave for twenty years, from 1852 to 1872. Today a statue of "Greyfriars Bobby" stands near the place where the real Bobby waited for so long.

Small dogs can also be funny. Some are trained to do funny things in movies and TV shows. Others learn on their own. A Lhasa apso named Nathan would rub his face on the carpet until the hair stuck out every which way. (His owners called it a "Nathan face.") Then he would strut

People come from all over the world to see this statue of Greyfriars Bobby. It honors the little dog who waited so long at his master's grave.

around until somebody noticed him and laughed.

"Make a Nathan face," they would say, and the little dog started his rubbing. If the first face didn't get a laugh, Nathan tried again. He kept trying until everybody was laughing.

Magic Dogs

In the Ryukyu Islands of Japan, some people believed that dogs had magic powers. A dog could leave its body as a spirit that no one could see or hear. When the dog's body died, the homeless spirit went to live in the body of a wizard. Such wizards were feared by the people, for it was said that the dog-spirit gave them great power.

Mixed breeds make loving pets. Cockapoos like this one are especially popular.

BEST BUDS: Size is no problem for friends. This miniature schnauzer weighs less than most six-month-old babies. His "bud" is a Great Dane who outweighs many grown men.

Small dogs

can be **purebred** or **mixed breed**. Some breeds are familiar, such as the poodle and dachshund (DOX-und); some are less familiar, such as the Japanese Chin and the Dandie Dinmont. There are also many types of mixed breeds that make fine companions.

All dogs share a common ancestry with the wolf, the jackal, the coyote (ki-O-te), and the fox. These wild members of the dog family range in size from a fennec fox that could fit into a sweater pocket to a timber wolf as big as a full-grown man. They live in many different **habitats**. Some live in the frozen northland, some in grasslands or deserts, some in steaming tropical forests.

Dogs have been companions to human beings for fourteen thousand years. This long friendship probably started with cave dwellers who took wolf pups and tried to tame them.

These tiny fennec foxes live in deserts. Their big ears help keep them cool.

Over time, the descendants of these tamed wolves became more and more doglike. Then different breeds began to appear.

Today there are hundreds of different breeds and mixed breeds. The American Kennel Club (AKC), an organization that keeps records on purebred dogs, recognizes one hundred forty breeds. They are grouped into seven categories: sporting, hound, working, terrier, toy, nonsporting, and herding.

The small breeds are found mostly in the toy and terrier groups, though a few are in other classes. For example, Lhasa apsos are classed as nonsporting, and the miniature dachshund is a small hound.

Wire-haired dachshunds have short legs and long bodies, like their smooth-coated cousins.

Lhasa apsos are one of the most popular of the Asian breeds. As family pets, they are cute and fun.

13

Members of the terrier group were first bred to hunt rats and other **vermin**. They are sturdy, healthy, affectionate—and stubborn. Terriers love to chase and to dig. If there is a way to get under the backyard fence, a terrier will find it. Raising and training one of these delightful little dogs takes patience. A strong, high fence won't hurt, either.

One of the oldest terrier breeds is the cairn. The breed comes from the Scottish Highlands. Cairns have wiry coats and bright eyes. They bounce when they walk, and love affection from their humans. Offshoots of the cairn are the Scottish terrier ("Scottie") and the West Highland white ("Westie"). Other small terriers include the Skye, the Norfolk, and the miniature schnauzer (SHNAU-zer).

Pomeranians are pert and pretty. They like lots of attention from their human friends.

West Highland white terriers are cheerful bundles of energy. They love to play with toys and explore their world.

(Dog) Show Business

Poodles are natural performers. They learn quickly and are not shy in crowds. This one is carefully groomed for a dog show.

Many people like to show off their dogs. The AKC and other groups hold contests in which dogs can win prizes and ribbons. In dog shows, dogs are judged against standards for their breed. Judges look at bone structure, the shape of the head, the condition of the coat, and many other things. The dog that comes closest to the breed standard wins "best of breed." In *obedience trials,* looks are not important. Dogs are judged by how well they obey commands like "come!" "sit!" "stay!" Both events draw many entries and also many fans, who come to see their favorite breeds in action.

Unlike the terriers, toy dogs were not bred to work, they were bred to be pets. They are small and pretty, but they are also remarkably hardy. Toy breeds often live well into their late teens. Many toy dogs are smaller versions of large breeds. The graceful Italian greyhound is a cousin of the large, racing

Miniature dachshunds are gentle and loving. Like the larger hound breeds, they have big, sad eyes.

greyhounds. The Pomeranian is related to the powerful sled dogs of the arctic, and the miniature pinscher to the fearsome Doberman.

There are many other small purebreds, and each has its fans. So do the mixed breeds. There are dozens of mixes, from Westie and Lhasa apso to Chihuahua and Pomeranian. The "poos" are especially popular. A poo is a cross between a poodle and another breed. There are cockapoos, Lhasapoos, shitzipoos, and more. Any of these purebreds or mixes can make a wonderful pet for the right family

Some people say that the Chihuahua has the looks of a fawn and the heart of a lion. "We forgot to tell her she's tiny," said one owner, as her Chihuahua barked furiously at a passing stranger.

Unclipped poodles look very different from show dogs with their "poodle cuts." This one enjoys a bus ride in Paris, France.

Most

dogs can live indoors quite happily, but they do not take well to being left alone for long periods. They like to stay close to their favorite human and to be the center of everyone's attention. A dog that feels ignored can become restless and destructive. This is especially true of the active little terriers.

Small dogs still behave like dogs. They bark at strangers, growl when they're angry, wag their tails when they're happy. If you pester them, they may bite. If you ignore them, they may chew the furniture. Their senses of hearing and smell are better than ours.

Dogs hear sounds that are too high-pitched for human ears. This is why they react to "silent" whistles. They also can tell the difference between familiar sounds and strange ones. They bark when a strange car pulls into the driveway or strange footsteps come to the door. They don't bark when it's the family car in the driveway or a familiar friend at the door.

Dogs have an excellent sense of smell. The **canine** nose is

Jack Russell terriers love a good chase. They will track a gopher into its hole, run the neighbor's cat out of the yard, and play fetch with anybody who will throw a stick or a ball. These two puppies look ready for anything.

lined with nerve endings that respond to odors. This is why dogs are forever sniffing at things. It is how they gather information about their world.

Dogs are good communicators. They express themselves with barks, whines, growls, yowls, and whimpers. Every dog

The Pembroke Welsh corgi is the smallest of the herding breeds. Corgi means "dwarf dog" in the Welsh language.

21

Two friends share a quiet time together. The dog is a Jack Russell terrier.

owner knows the difference between a bark of greeting and a bark of warning. The same thing is true for growls. Nobody would confuse a threatening growl with the noisy rumblings of puppies playing tug-of-war.

Body language is another way that dogs communicate. Ears up means the dog is paying attention; ears forward means it's on the alert. When a dog bares its teeth and growls, it is making a threat. When it bares its teeth and does not growl, watch out! It is ready to attack.

A dog's tail has a language of its own. A wagging tail means the dog is happy. A drooping tail means it's upset or sick. A tail tucked between the legs means it's afraid.

Many dogs can even "tell time" — that is, they learn when certain things should be done. They know when it's time to get up and when it's time to leave for work or school. They know when it's time to come home. If someone is late, the dog may fret and whimper until that person returns.

Chinese pugs can look funny and fierce at the same time. The dark mask and downturned mouth are important features of the breed.

Why Dogs Pant

Dogs do not perspire as humans do. When a human gets too hot, sweating cools the body. When a dog gets too hot, it hangs its tongue out of its mouth and pants. Air moving over the wet tongue helps to cool it. Panting does not work as well as sweating. That is why it is dangerous to leave a dog in a hot car. On hot summer days, small dogs have been known to die of heatstroke in less than an hour.

Puppies love to be cuddled. Holding and petting help build the bond between a dog and its owner.

Small dogs

always seem to be on somebody's lap or curled up near humans. They "watch" TV, play with anybody who is willing, and grumble if they feel left out of anything. Caring for these special pets is an important job.

Dogs need fresh water every day, and good, nutritious food. It can be canned, dry, or a mix of both. Puppies need to eat small meals four to six times a day. Adult dogs usually do fine with once-a-day feedings. They also can have treats, especially chewy ones like rawhide sticks or hard dog biscuits. Chewing helps keep a dog's teeth clean.

Many small dogs like "human" food. There is no reason they can't have scraps of meat, eggs, and vegetables as part of their regular diet. Just don't let the dog eat too much.

A graceful papillon waits for a treat. See how the fringed ears seem to "flow" back from the face.

25

Dogs need good, nourishing food in the right amounts. A dog that eats too much will get fat. Being overweight is no better for dogs than it is for people.

Being fat can shorten your pet's life. Do not give your dog sweets like cookies, cake, or candy. Sugar not only makes dogs fat—it rots their teeth.

Your dog needs a warm bed and a place to go to the bathroom. Some small dogs are "paper trained." They go to the bathroom on a paper in the laundry room or on the service porch. Others go outside. Either way, your dog's toilet area should be cleaned at least once a day.

Your pet also must be kept clean. All dogs need regular brushing and occasional baths. They need to have their ears washed and their toenails clipped. Some owners like to do this at home. Others take the dog to a professional groomer.

Medical care is also important. Dogs need shots to protect them against certain diseases. A **veterinarian** can explain what shots your dog needs and when it should have them.

There is one other thing

Regular visits to the veterinarian are important for your dog. This one-year-old cairn terrier is having his annual checkup.

The Dog That Went Over the Rainbow

One of the most famous dogs in the world exists only in a story. Toto, Dorothy's little black dog in *The Wizard of Oz*, was a happy-go-lucky terrier that loved to play. Author L. Frank Baum described Toto as "a little black dog, with long silky hair and small black eyes that twinkled merrily on either side of his funny, wee nose. Toto played all day long, and Dorothy played with him, and loved him dearly."

Puppies spend most of their time sleeping, eating, or playing. This Norfolk terrier looks like it just woke up from a nice long nap.

every dog must have: love and attention. Play with your dog. Dogs love ear scratches and tummy rubs. They do not like being teased, poked, or hit. Be gentle when you play. Taking care of your small friend will not always be fun and sunshine. Nobody likes to clean up potty papers or pick burrs out of a tail.

These special pets have a way of making it all worthwhile. They love without question, and will gladly be your friend for life.

Games Little Dogs Play

Part of the fun of dog ownership is playing with your four-legged friend. Small dogs can enjoy many games. Tug-of-war is a favorite of many. Make a soft "rope" by braiding old socks, and tie a fat knot at each end. Get your dog to grab on, and the fun begins. Don't pull too hard, though; just *pretend* to be pulling hard.

"Fetch" is another popular game, especially with terriers. Chasing a ball, a stick, or a Frisbee will keep many a small dog happy for hours. Some dogs enjoy learning "tricks." They will jump over a stick or dance on their hind legs or speak on command. Be patient and gentle in teaching tricks; the experience should be fun, not a chore.

Fun Facts

- There are 27 million pet dogs in the United States.

- North Americans spend billions of dollars a year on medical care for their pets.

- The smallest dog in the *Guiness Book of World Records* is a Yorkshire terrier about the size of a hamster.

- Dogs have forty-two teeth.

- Puppies develop inside their mothers for sixty-two to sixty-three days. Average litter size is three to six puppies.

- Toy breeds were the dogs of European royalty. Tiny papillons appear in fifteenth-century paintings of French nobles. Queen Victoria of England owned several Pomeranians.

- Dogs have three eyelids: an upper, a lower, and an inner lid. The inner lid sweeps across the eye from the inside corner, acting like a windshield wiper.

- Some dogs have two coats: an outer covering of rough hair and an inner one that is silky and furlike.

Glossary

breed: A group of animals that share the same ancestry, basic characteristics, and appearance.

canine: Of or belonging to the dog family of animals.

habitat: The area or kind of environment in which an animal normally lives.

mixed breed: A dog whose parents were not of the same breed.

purebred: A dog whose parents and ancestors were of the same breed.

vermin: Small animals regarded as harmful, such as rats and gophers.

veterinarian: A doctor who takes care of animals.

Find Out More About Small Dogs

American Kennel Club. *The Complete Dog Book for Kids*. New York: Howell Book House, 1996.

Brock, Juliet Clutton. *Dog*. New York: Alfred A. Knopf, 1991.

Brown, Marc Tolon. *Arthur's New Puppy*. New York: Little Brown, 1993.

Evans, Mark. *ASPCA Pet Care Guide for Kids: Puppy*. New York: Dorling Kindersley, 1993.

Petty, Kate. *Dogs* (First Pets series). New York: Barron's Juveniles, 1993.

White, Nancy. *Why Do Dogs Do That?* New York: Scholastic, 1995.

About the Author

Linda Jacobs Altman lives in the small town of Clearlake, California. She and her husband, Richard, share their home with three dogs, four cats, and two cockatiels. Ms. Altman has written many books for young people, including a history of the California Gold Rush and a book about women inventors.